READING FUN WITH WITH WORD FAMILIES

BOBBIE LAVENDER

Copyright © 2021 by Bobbie Lavender

All rights reserved. No part of this publication may be reproduced, distributed, or transmitted in any form or by any means, including photocopying, recording, or other electronic or mechanical methods, without the prior written permission of the publisher, except in the case brief quotations embodied in critical reviews and other noncommercial uses permitted by copyright law.

ISBN: 978-1-63945-097-8 (Paperback)

The views expressed in this book are solely those of the author and do not necessarily reflect the views of the publisher, and the publisher hereby disclaims any responsibility for them.

Writers' Branding
1800-608-6550
www.writersbranding.com
orders@writersbranding.com

Contents

ACKNOWLEDGMENTS	ix
STORY #1	1
STORY #2	2
STORY #3	3
STORY #4	4
STORY #5	5
STORY #6	6
STORY #7	7
STORY #8	8
STORY #9	9
STORY #10	10
STORY #11	11
STORY #12	12
STORY #13	13
STORY #14	14
STORY #15	15
STORY #16	16
STORY #17	17
STORY #18	18
STORY #19	19
STORY #20	20
STORY #21	21
STORY #22	22
STORY #23	23
STORY #24	24
STORY #25	25
STORY #26	26
STORY #27	27
STORY #28	28
STORY #29	29
STORY #30	30
STORY #31	31
STORY #32	32
STORY #33	33
STORY #34	34
STORY #35	35
STORY #36	36

STORY #37	37
STORY #38	38
STORY #47	39
STORY #49	40
STORY #41	41
STORY #42	42
STORY #43	43
STORY #44	44
STORY #45	45
STORY #46	46
STORY #47	47
STORY #48	48
STORY #58	49
STORY #50	50
STORY #51	51
STORY #52	52
STORY #53	53
STORY #54	54
STORY #55	55
STORY #56	56
STORY #57	57
STORY #58	58
STORY #59	59
STORY #60	60
STORY #61	61
STORY #62	62
STORY #63	63
STORY #64	64
STORY #65	65
STORY #66	66
STORY #67	67
STORY #68	68
STORY #69	69
STORY #70	70
STORY #71	71
STORY #72	72
STORY #73	73
STORY #74	74
STORY #75	75
STORY #76	76
STORY #77	77

STORY #78 78
STORY #79 79
STORY #80 80
STORY #81 81
STORY #82 82
STORY #83 83
STORY #84 84
STORY #85 85
STORY #86 86
STORY #87 87
STORY #88 88
STORY #89 89
STORY #90 90
STORY #91 91
STORY #92 92
STORY #93 93
STORY #94 94
STORY #95 95
STORY #96 96
STORY #97 97
STORY #98 98
STORY #99 99
STORY #100 100

In memory of my son, Robert Reynaud Lavender. This book is dedicated to my daughter, Robbie Lavender Nichols. Story 100 is dedicated to my husband, Charles C. Lavender.

ACKNOWLEDGMENTS

I would like to thank my family and friends who gave me encouragement and helped in making the publication of this book become a reality. The sole purpose of this work is to help children read. Maybe this source will encourage children to be life-long readers.

Special thanks are extended to the following:

Nancy Simmons, Mary Bosen and Bunny Petty...editing.

Michael Unanue... technical advising.

Burkley and Charlie Elizabeth Nichols (granddaughters) for critiquing the stories.

Donna Thomas for her testimonies, persistence, and encouragement in ensuring the publication of this book.

And to all my acquaintances who share my enthusiasm for helping children learn to read.

STORY #1

REVIEW and NEW WORDS

At

Cat   is
Fat   a
Scat   my

SCAT

Scat is a cat.
Scat is my cat.
Scat is fat.
Scat is my fat cat.
Is Scat a fat cat?   YES   NO
Scat is my fat cat.
Is Scat my fat cat?   YES   NO

STORY #2

REVIEW and NEW WORDS

At
Cat   the
Pat   is
Fat   a
Scat

THE CAT

Pat the cat. Pat the fat cat. The fat cat is Scat. Scat is the fat cat. Pat the fat cat. Pat, pat, pat, the fat cat, Scat. Pat the fat cat.

Scat is the fat cat. Pat, pat, pat, Scat the fat cat. Is the fat cat Scat?

YES   NO

STORY #3

At   REVIEW and NEW WORDS

At   with
Cat   is
Scat   at
Hat   the
Bat   can
Rat
Nat

SCAT

Scat is a cat. Scat is a cat with a hat. Scat is a cat with a hat at bat with Nat the rat.

Scat the cat can bat. Nat the rat can bat. Can the hat bat?

STORY #4

At   REVIEW and NEW WORDS

Cat   on
Pat   is
Nat   the
Sat   yes
Scat   no
Fat
Mat

A CAT ON A MAT

A cat is on a mat. The cat on the mat is fat.

Is the cat fat? The cat is fat. Is the cat Scat? The cat on the mat is Scat.

Scat is on the mat. A fat cat sat on a mat. The fat cat is Scat.

Pat the mat, fat cat. Scat is on the mat. Is the mat on Scat?

YES   NO

STORY #5

At REVIEW and NEW WORDS

Scat not
Cat   is
Fat   on
Nat
Hat
Pat
Rat
Mat
Sat

A HAT

A hat is on the cat. The cat is on the mat. Scat is a cat. Nat is a rat.

A cat is on a hat. Pat the hat.

Nat sat on the hat. Is the hat on Nat? The hat is not on Nat. Nat is on the hat.

A hat is on a cat. A hat is on Scat the cat.

Is the hat on the mat?	YES	NO
Is the cat on the hat?	YES	NO
Is the mat on the cat?	YES	NO

The hat is on Scat the cat.

STORY #6

At   REVIEW and NEW WORDS

At   look
Sat   not
Fat   draw
Rat
Nat
Bat
Pat
Hat
Mat

LOOK AT NAT

Look at Nat bat. Look at Nat the rat bat the mat. Nat is at bat.

Look at the hat on the rat. The rat sat on the hat. Look, look, look. Look at the hat.

Look at the fat cat, Scat. Look at the rat on the mat. The rat is not fat.

Scat, the cat is fat. Look at the fat cat.

Draw a fat cat.

Draw a rat.

STORY #7

En REVIEW and NEW WORDS

Ten	in
Hen	sit
Pen	nest
Ben	lay
	eggs
	for
	can
	like
	I

TEN HENS

Ten hens can sit. Ten hens can sit on a nest in a pen. Ten hens can sit on a nest in a pen and lay ten eggs for Ben. I like hens

I like eggs.

I like Ben.

STORY #8

En	REVIEW and NEW WORDS
Jen	and
Ben	count
Pen	to
Ten	lay
Den	eggs
like	
draw	

JEN THE HEN

Jen is a hen. Look at Jen and Ben. Look at Jen and Ben in the hen pen.

Look at the hen pen. Look at the den.

A hen pen is not a den. Jen is in the hen pen. Ben is in the den. Ben can count to ten. Jen can lay ten eggs. Look at the eggs. Count the eggs.

I like Jen and Ben. I like eggs. I like to count to ten. Draw a hen pen.

Draw hens in the pen.

STORY #9

En REVIEW and NEW WORDS

Jen	do
Ben	little
Ken	has
Men	big
Ten	see
Den	blue
	black
	red
	yellow
	green
	brown

JEN THE RED HEN

Jen is a red hen. She lays brown eggs. Ken is a black rat. He has ten yellow hats.

Ten men in the pen see Jen. I see ten men with Jen, Ben and Ken, in the pen.

The pen is big and blue. The den is little and green.

Look at the pen.

Look at the den.

Ben and Ken like Jen.

I like Jen, the little red hen.

Do you like Jen, the little red hen?

STORY #10

En   REVIEW and NEW WORDS

When	you
Then	and
Ten	in
Men	are
	to
	count

JEN CAN COUNT

When can Jen count to ten? When Ben counts to ten, then Jen can count to ten.

Ben is in the pen when Jen is in the pen. Ben and Jen are in the pen.

When can I count? When Ben and Jen count, then you can count to ten with all the men.

Ben can count to ten. Jen can count to ten. All the men can count to ten.

Can you count to ten? Yes, I can count to ten.

I like to count to ten.

I like to count to ten with Ben and Jen.

STORY #11

Ug   REVIEW and NEW WORDS

Bug   will
Dug   hole
Rug   that

BUGS

A big bug.

A little bug.

A big bug and a little bug dug a hole in the rug.

Will you hug the bugs? No, I will not hug the bugs that dug a hole in the rug.

STORY #12

Ug   REVIEW and NEW WORDS

Mug	funny	red
Jug	one	blue
Hug	two	green
Dug	three	
Bug	has	
	draw	
	thank	
	you	
	that	

THE FUNNY BUG

The funny big red bug sits on the blue rug. He has a little green mug. He likes to hug.

Will you hug the funny big red bug that has the little green mug and sits on the blue rug?

No, I will not hug the funny big red bug that sits on the blue rug, has a green mug, and likes to hug.

Draw a red bug.

Draw a blue rug.

Draw a green mug.

Thank you.

STORY #13

Ug   REVIEW and NEW WORDS

Zug   dog
Pug   they
Slug   end
Tug
Jug
Lug
Hug

ZUG AND PUG

Zug is a bug. Pug is a dog. Zug and Pug tug at the rug.

Zug dug for a slug. Pug dug for a slug. Look at the slug. The slug is in the jug. Pug and Zug cannot lug the slug in the jug to the rug.

Pug has a mug.

Zug has a mug.

Pug and Zug, with their mugs, are snug on the rug.

They hug.

The end.

STORY #14

Og   REVIEW and NEW WORDS

Frog	know
Bog	lives
Log	that
	sits
	oops
	happened
	there
	goes
	off
	what

FROG

I know a green frog. I know a green frog that lives in a bog and sits on a log. The log is big. The green frog is little.

Oops! There goes the frog off the log.

Do you know what happened?

Draw what happened.

STORY #15

Og   REVIEW and NEW WORDS

Frog	yes
Bog	ha, ha, ha
Jog	they
Tog	fall
Fog	poor
	he
	pig
	happy
	sob

FROG AND TOG

Frog is a little green frog. Tog is a big brown dog. Frog likes Tog. Tog likes Frog.

Frog and Tog can jog on a big log. They cannot see in the fog. They fall off the log into the bog. Poor, poor Frog and Tog. Sob, sob, sob.

I see a fat hog in the bog. He likes the bog. Yes, yes, yes. A hog is a pig.

Ha, ha, ha. He is a happy hog in the bog.

Draw a big happy hog.

STORY #16

Og   REVIEW and NEW WORDS

Frog	can	black
Jog	see	red
Tog	sit	brown
Log	bark	green
Hog	roll	
Bog	happy	
Dog	eat	

CAN YOU SEE?

Can you see the frog? He is little and green. Can you see the log? It is big and black. The frog likes to sit on the log.

Can you see the dog? He is little and brown. He likes to jog. He can bark and jog on the log.

Can you see the hog? He is red and fat. He likes to eat and roll in the bog. He is a happy hog in the bog.

STORY #17

An   REVIEW and NEW WORDS

Dan	she	girl
Van	has	color
Man	black	
Tan	he	
Jan	and	
Pan	have	
Fan	sun	
Nan		

DAN THE MAN

Dan is a man. Dan is in a van. Dan likes the sun. Dan, the man, is a tan man. Dan likes Nan. Nan likes Dan.

Nan has a fan. Nan has a little blue fan. She can fan.

Jan is a girl. Nan is a girl. Dan is a man. Jan, Nan, and Dan have a big black pan.

Draw a big pan and color it black.

The End.

STORY #18

REVIEW and NEW WORDS

An	
Dan	with
Nan	likes
Can	he
Van	down
Tan	hill
Man	little
Jan	draw

DAN AND THE VAN

Dan ran the big red van down the green hill.

Draw a green hill.

Nan and Jan can see Dan, the man, in the big red van.

Draw a big red van.

Dan can see a little black pan. Dan sits on a tan mat in the van with the little black pan. He likes his big red van and his little black pan.

Draw a little black pan.

STORY #19

III   REVIEW and NEW WORDS

Will   lives
Hill   works
Mill   boxes
Fill   toys
Bill   for
Jill   top
Thrill

WILL

Will lives on a hill and works at the mill. Will lives on a hill and works at the mill to fill boxes of toys for Bill and Jill, who live on top of the hill. Will, Bill and Jill live on top of the hill. It is a thrill to live on top of the hill.

STORY #20

III   REVIEW and NEW WORDS

Bill	loves	dolls
Will	are	four
Jill	boys	car
Hill	play	has
Mill	toys	up
Fill	ball	
Spill	too	
Still	not	

BILL and WILL

Bill and Will are boys. They like toys. Bill has a big blue ball. Will has a little yellow car. See the big blue ball. See the little yellow car. Bill and Will go up the hill to the mill. They fill the van with toys for all the little girls and boys. They do not spill the toys.

Jill is a little girl. She likes toys too. She still likes to play with dolls. She has little dolls and big dolls. She has one, two, three, four dolls. She likes to play with her dolls. She loves her dolls.

STORY #21

ILL   REVIEW and NEW WORDS

Bill	see	on	oh
Jill	colors	they	
Will	up	fun	
Spill	down	have	
	go	with	
	yellow	brown	
	green	for	

BILL CAN SEE JILL

Bill can see Jill. Jill can see Bill. Bill and Jill will go up the big hill. They will fill the can with colors. They will not spill the colors in the can. They will go down the hill. Oh, what fun it is to go up and down the hill with Bill and Jill.

Bill can color a cat. Jill can color a cat and a rat.

Bill and Jill will have fun. They will go up and down the hill. They will color.

Bill can see Jill on the green hill. Jill can see Bill go down the green hill.

Draw a green hill for Bill and Jill.

STORY #22

Op   REVIEW and NEW WORDS

Hop   of
Top   and
Stop   lollypop
Pop   good
        from
        get

HOP

Hop to the top. Hop to the top of the hill. Hop to the top of the hill and stop the cop with the lollypop.

The lollypop is red. The lollypop is good. Get a lollypop from the cop on top of the hill.

STORY #23

Op   REVIEW and NEW WORDS

Hop	bunny		poor
Hoppy	on		purple
Stop	said		
Top	went		
Cop	off		
Mop	now		
Flop	of		

HOPPY CAN HOP

Hoppy is a bunny. He can hop, hop, hop. Hoppy can hop and stop. "Stop Hoppy, stop, stop, stop" said the cop.

Hoppy can hop on top of the mop. Flop, went Hoppy off the top of the mop. Poor Hoppy, the mop is now on top of Hoppy.

Draw a brown bunny.

Draw a red and purple mop on top of Hoppy.

Funny, funny, bunny.

STORY #24

Op   REVIEW and NEW WORDS

Drop	happy	of
Flop	said	fast
Pop	went	not
Drop	with	sits
Bop	car	up
Mop	run	go
Stop	has	do

THE COP and THE RAT

The cop has a blue car. The cop sits on top of the blue car. He can see Bill with a mop. He can see Bill bop the rat with the mop. Run, rat, run.

Stop, Bill stop. Bill has a mop. Run, rat, run. "Stop," said the cop. Bop, goes Bill with the mop. Flop, goes the rat. Pop up and go, rat. Go fast. Do not stop, rat. Hop on top of the car with the cop and go fast.

Happy little rat.

STORY #25

Ig   REVIEW and NEW WORDS

Mig	cutest
Pig	dance
Big	sing
Wig	her
Jiggy	pink
Jig	

MIG

Mig is a pig. Mig is a pig with the cutest big red wig. She can sing and dance a "Jiggy Jig" in her cute big red wig.

Draw a pink pig in a red wig.

STORY #26

Ig   REVIEW and NEW WORDS

Mig	put
Pig	do
Big	can
Wig	sees
Jig	on
Dig	make
Fig	tree
Zig	for

SEE MIG THE PIG

See Mig, the little pig, in the big red wig. See Mig, the little pig, in the big red wig do a jig. Funny, funny little pig.

Draw a little pig with a big red wig.

Mig the pig, can dig for a big fig. She can zig and dig and do a jig. She sees a fig on a big fig tree.

Draw a big green fig tree. Put figs on the tree.

STORY #27

ig   REVIEW and NEW WORDS

Rig	Dan	they	truck
Big	Dan's	funny	very
Wig	blue	his	will
Wigs	green	go	likes
Jig	and	you	are
		with	
		hit	
		stop	

DAN'S RIG

Dan, the man, has a big blue rig and a green wig. A rig is a very big truck. He can go fast in his big blue rig with his big green wig. Dan, the man, is funny.

Stop; see the pig. Do not go fast in the big blue rig. You will hit the pig.

Draw a pig and a rig.

Dan can stop the big rig. He likes the pig. The pig and Dan can do a jig with green wigs. They are funny. Dan is big. The pig is little.

Draw big Dan and the little pig.

STORY #28

Et   REVIEW and NEW WORDS

Get	fly	said
Ret	friends	you
Let	duck	high
Met	who	sky
Fret	come	fun
Chet	take	
Jet	ride	
Wet	us	

RET and CHET

Ret and Chet are friends. Ret and Chet like to fly in jets. They met a wet duck who likes to fly in jets.

"Come, take a ride with us," said Ret and Chet. "We will let you get the jet high in the sky. Do not fret. It will be fun to ride in the jet."

STORY #29

Et   REVIEW and NEW WORDS

Bet	rabbit
Bet's	go
Get	on
Jet	not
Let	still
Met	you
Net	silly
Pet	
Set	
Wet	
Yet	
Vet	

BET'S PET

Bet is a boy. Bet has one black pet. Bet has one black rabbit for a pet. Bet's pet can get wet. Let me see Bet's wet pet. The wet pet and the wet net are on the vet's jet.

Can the pet go on the jet? No, not yet, he is still wet. Let me pet the wet rabbit. No, not yet, he will get you wet. Silly wet pet.

STORY #30

Et   REVIEW and NEW WORDS

Fret	him
Chet	name
Wet	toy
Met	fish
Let	have
Let's	fun
Get	play
Net	mom
Pet	said
Jet	was
Set	
Sets	

CHET

Let me get the wet pig in a big net. Stop, you cannot get a pig in a big net. Do not fret; the pig will let me get him in the big net.

He is a pet pig. His name is Chet. He is fun. He has a toy wet set and a wet fish net. We have fun with his toy wet set. A wet set is water toys. Let's go play with the toy wet set and get wet. I like to get wet. Do you?

I met Mom. I was wet. She did not fret. She said it was funny. Let's all get wet with Chet.

STORY #31

Ell   REVIEW and NEW WORDS

Bell	love	eat
Tell	have	his
Sell	hamster	dinner
Smell	my	or
	ring	time

MY HAMSTER

I have a little hamster. I have a little hamster that can smell. I have a little hamster that can smell and ring a bell.

My hamster can tell when it is time to eat.

When it is time to eat, he rings a little bell, and I can tell it is his dinner time.

I will not sell my little hamster. I will not sell his bell. I love my little hamster.

STORY #32

Ell   REVIEW and NEW WORDS

Chell   girls
Nell   friends
Shell   from
Yell   sea
Bell   when
Spell   ring
Jell   what
Jell-O
Tell

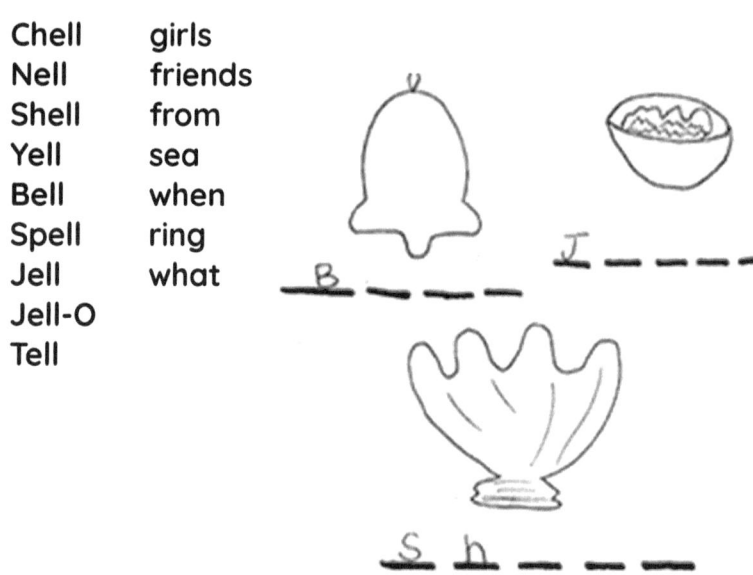

CHELL and NELL

Chell and Nell are girls. They are friends. They like to get shells. They have big shells and little shells. They get the shells from the sea. Do you have shells from the sea?

They yell and ring a bell when they get a shell. They can spell <u>Shell</u>, <u>Bell</u> and <u>Jell-O</u>.

They like shells and red Jell-O. Do you like shells and Jell-O? Tell me what color of Jell-O you like.

STORY #33

Ell   REVIEW and NEW WORDS

Dell	hello	them
Fell	Jell-O	get
Tell	yellow	said
Sell	mellow	more
Well	Nelly	got
Shell	name	out
Yell	about	good-bye

NELLY

Hello, my name is Nelly. I will tell you about the bell and the shell. The bell and the shell fell into the well. I got them out. The yellow shell and the blue shell said, "Thank you."

I gave them yellow, mellow Jell-O to eat. They liked it. They will tell Mom to get more yellow, mellow Jell-O. I will tell the man to sell her more yellow, mellow Jell-O.

The bell and the shell are happy to tell you that they are well. They will have fun down in the green dell.

Good-bye, bell.

Good-bye, shell.

STORY #34

Ub   REVIEW and NEW WORDS

Rub	cute	chubby
Scrub	with	tubby
Cub	but	Bubba
Club	ride	
Sub	under	
Stub	sea	
Tub	have	

BUBBA

Bubba is a cute little cub with a stub nose. He likes to rub, rub, rub and scrub, scrub, scrub with his little club in his big tub.

Yes, he is chubby. Yes, he is tubby, but he can ride in a sub under the sea and have fun. Cute little chubby Bubba has a cute little snub nose.

STORY #35

Ub   REVIEW and NEW WORDS

Cub	that	goes	sandwich
Hub	and	only	boat
Rub	orange	down	
Sub	my	good	
Tub	eat	all	
Stub	has	day	
Scrub	toy I	ong	

MY CUB

I have a cub that can rub and scrub in the big orange tub. He likes to scrub and rub all day long.

My cub can eat a sub sandwich. It is a good sub sandwich. I like subs too.

My cub has a toy sub. It is a toy boat. When his sub goes down, you can only see a stub of the sub in the tub. Funny little sub boat.

STORY #36

Ice REVIEW and NEW WORDS

Ice	cold	shake
Nice	sweet	cone
Lice	float	bowl
Mice	know	milk
Rice	what	comes
Dice	what	many
Slice	cream	flavors
Spice	scream	favorite
Twice	just	
Price	stick	

ICE CREAM

It is cold. It is sweet. It is good. Do you know what it is? It is ice cream. I just love ice cream.

I can eat it on a stick. I can eat it in a cone or a bowl. I can eat an ice cream sandwich. I can make an ice cream float or a milk shake. Ice cream comes in many flavors. What is your favorite flavor of ice cream?

"Ice cream, ice cream, we all scream for ice cream." Draw an ice cream cone.

STORY #37

Ice   REVIEW and NEW WORDS

Ice	thing	slide
Dice	life	fast
Mice	smile	
Nice	their	
Rice	hide	
Lice	your	
Twice	five	
Slice	want	
Spice	white	

THREE LITTLE MICE

The three little mice like to play on the white ice. They like to run and slide on the ice. They fall down twice on the ice. That is not a nice thing to do.

They see five lice. The mice run fast. They do not want lice. That is funny. Run mice, run and hide. Run for your life.

This time they play with dice and eat spice in their rice. That is nice.

They pile the spice on the rice and smile. They are funny little mice.

Smile twice, little mice.

STORY #38

Ice   REVIEW and NEW WORDS

Ice	cake	want
Spice	of	give
Lice	cream	five
Slice	say	scoops
Nice	white	this
Twice	icing	but
Rice	good	today
	Bye	

SPICE CAKE

I like spice cake. I will have a slice of spice cake and ice cream. That will be so nice. I like cake and ice cream. Can you say that twice?

The white icing can slide down the side of the spice cake. It is so good.

Give me five scoops of ice cream and a slice of spice cake. Yes, yes, yes. I will not eat rice this time. No, no, no. It is nice, but I have had rice twice today. I want spice cake and ice cream.

Thank you.

Good-bye.

STORY #47

Ate   REVIEW and NEW WORDS

Kate	strawberries	garden
Plate	served	does
Gate	pretty	snakes
Mate	play	still
Skate	dress-up	don't
Late	through	me

KATE, MY PLAYMATE

Kate is my playmate. We like to eat dates and strawberries served on a pretty plate.

We play "dress-up." I like Kate, and Kate likes me.

Nate is a boy. He comes through the garden gate to play with us. He does not like to play "dress-up." He likes cars, skates, and snakes. He likes to make us scream.

We still like Nate. He likes dates and strawberries served on a pretty plate.

Come play with us. Don't be late.

STORY #49

Ate REVIEW and NEW WORDS

Ate	by
Crate	was
Date	for
Gate	roller
Hate	ice
Late	clean
Plate	your
Bate	candy
Rate	put
Skate	hurry
Slate	

KATE

Kate sat the crate by the gate. She was late for her date. She hates to be late.

Kate likes to skate on slate by the gate. Do you like to skate? Can you roller skate? Can you ice skate?

Kate likes to eat. She has a clean plate. Eat your date on the plate. I like date candy. Mom made date candy for Kate and me. Do not be late, Kate. Run to the gate, Kate. Put the plate and the skates by the crate. Hurry Kate, do not be late for the date.

STORY #41

Ate   REVIEW and NEW WORDS

Ate	my
Crate	friend
Date	meet
Grate	at
Hate	fast
Late	would
Plate	stand
Rate	me
Skate	come
Slate	along

MY FRIEND KATE

Kate is my friend. We have fun. We have a date to meet at the gate to skate. I hate to be late. We like to skate. We skate at a fast rate. It is fun to skate with Kate.

Would you like to stand on the crate and see Kate and me skate on the slate by the gate? Come along. We will have a fun date on the skates.

STORY #42

Ate   REVIEW and NEW WORDS

Brick   black
Flick   bark
Trick   many
Slick   catch
Quick   air
Click   wink
Tick   eyes
Sick   wag
Pick   hand
Nick   really
Stick   tail

NICK and SLICK

Nick has a dog named Slick. Slick is a big black dog. He likes to have fun. He can do many tricks. He can catch a stick, bark at a brick and flick a ball in the air. He is quick as a wink. He can blink his eyes, wag his tail, and lick Nick's hand. Nick and Slick really click.

One day, Nick found a tick on Slick. Quick, get a stick and pick the tick off Slick. Ticks can make you sick.

No ticks on Slick now. We are all happy.

STORY #43

Ick   REVIEW and NEW WORDS

Chick	baby
Brick	cute
Flick	pop
Rick	doing
Lick	that
Pick	good-bye
Slick	out
Sick	shell
Nick	
Quick	
Trick	
Stick	
Wick	

THE CHICK

The baby chick is cute. He can pick at the egg shell and pop out. Out popped the chick!

The baby chick likes to pick at a brick and flick a stick. He is quick. He likes to run and kick a ball. See him go! See him do the run and kick trick. That is so cute. He is a quick slick chick doing that trick.

Good-bye, quick slick chick. Run, run, run as fast as you can, quick slick chick.

STORY #44

Ick   REVIEW and NEW WORDS

Mick	Quick	are
Brick	Rick	brothers
Chick	Sick	football
Flick	Tick	popsicles
Kick	Wick	cold
Lick	Trick	eat
Slick	apples	
Nick	from	
Pick	them	

RICK, NICK and MICK

Rick, Nick and Mick are brothers. They like to kick a football and lick popsicles. The popsicles are cold and slick. Quick, eat them! Rick can pick apples. Nick can flick a stick. Mick can see a tick. Rick, Nick and Mick do not like ticks. The ticks will make you sick. Quick, Rick, Nick and Mick, run from the ticks.

Can you pick up a stick? Can you pick up a chick? Can you pick up a brick?

Can you do three tricks? I can do one trick with a stick.

STORY #45

Ale   REVIEW and NEW WORDS

Dale	snail	their	slow
Gale	very	skin	slowly
Scale	move	slide	small
Whale	warm	race	hurry
days	along	large	
place	snow		

DALE and GALE, THE SNAILS

Dale and Gale are snails. They are very, very, very slow. They like warm days. They like wet places.

A whale is very large. A snail is very small. Snails do not have scales.

Their skin is wet and slick.

Dale and Gale like to slide along slowly. They do not like to race. They do not like snow. They just like to be snails and move along slowly.

Can you hurry, little snail? No, no, no, I am slow.

STORY #46

Ale   REVIEW and NEW WORDS

Bale	farm	that
Gale	farmer	of
Hale	hay	more
Male	live	
Pale	sea	
Sale	cows	
Scale	horses	
Stale	would	
Tale	some	
Whale		

FARMER DALE

Farmer Dale lives on a farm. He has a truck, and he can get a bale of hay.

He puts the bale of hay on a scale. It is as big as a whale!

Do whales eat hay? No, no, no, whales live in the sea. Cows and horses can eat a bale of hay.

A pale male horse would not eat the bale of stale hay. Farmer Dale did not like the stale hay. He got some more hay on sale. It was good. The pale male horse ate all of it.

That is a whale of a tale.

The End

STORY #47

Ale   REVIEW and NEW WORDS

Bale	are	believe
Gale	sister	
Hale	brother	
Male	tell	
Pale	tall	
Sale	told	
Scale	about	
Stale	who	
Tale	wow	
Whale	was	

DALE and GALE

Dale and Gale are brother and sister. Dale is a boy. Gale is a girl. Dale likes to tell tall tales. Gale likes to go to sales.

Dale told a tale about a male whale who got on a scale. Wow, he was big. He was as big as 100 bales! Do you believe Dale?

Gale went to a sale. She got a toy pale whale. He was little and did not make a gale. She likes to play with the pale whale in the tub. Do you believe Gale?

STORY #48

Uck   REVIEW and NEW WORDS

Duck	Ducky	feather
Buck	chickens	wing
Truck	sweet	don't
Stuck	yellow	know
Cluck	quack	maybe
Luck	swim	
Pluck	under	
Yuck	water	

DUCKY

Ducky is not a chicken. He is a sweet little yellow duck. Can he cluck? No, but he can quack. He is a duck. He can swim and duck under the water. He looks for bugs…..YUCK! Will he eat the bugs? I don't know; maybe he will. Yuck, yuck, yuck, I do not eat bugs. Do you?

Ducky looks for his mother. She is a duck too. She loves her little Ducky duck. Ducky's mother plucked a feather from her wing and gave it to Ducky. Ducky is a lucky duck.

STORY #49

Uck   REVIEW and NEW WORDS

Buck	found	other
Bucky	white	
Chuck	bone	
Clucky	before	
Duck	could	
Ducky	now	
Luck	six	
Lucky	boo-hoo	
Hucky	rich	
Pluck	ok	
Struck	gives	
Truck	some	

LUCKY, THE DOG

Lucky is a lucky dog. He found a big white bone. Before he could get his bone, a big green truck struck his bone. Now, he has six little bones.

Boo-hoo.

That is ok. He will give some bones to his friends. He is lucky. He has four friends. He gives one bone to Bucky, one bone to Ducky, one bone to Chucky and one bone to Hucky. The other two bones are for Lucky. He is a lucky dog. He has two bones and four friends. What luck! He struck it rich with friends. He is a happy, lucky dog. Do you have a pet dog?

STORY #50

Uck   REVIEW and NEW WORDS

Buck	quack	deer
Chuck	named	really
Cluck	Chicky	play
Duck	Dicky	chicken
Luck	sometimes	purple
Lucky	their	
Pluck	feathers	
Struck	pretty	
Truck	find	
Ducky	next	

LUCKY DUCKY and CHICKY DICKY

Lucky Ducky is a yellow duck. She can quack. She has a friend named Chicky Dicky. Chicky Dicky is a chicken, and she can cluck. Lucky Ducky and Chicky Dicky quack and cluck all day. Sometimes they pluck their feathers. They have pretty feathers.

One day, they find a purple and orange toy truck. What luck! The next day, they find a brown buck. A buck is a male deer. They are really lucky. Now, they can play with the truck and the buck and quack and cluck all day.

STORY #51

Ing   REVIEW and NEW WORDS

Sing	song	what
Thing	pretty	along
Ring	fills	march
Rings	air	
Spring	joy	
Wing	happiness	
Wings	sometimes	
Bring	flap	
Fling	drum	

SING A SONG

Sing a song along with me. What a pretty thing it is to sing a song. It fills the air with joy and happiness. It sometimes rings in spring. The birds sing as they flap their wings in the air.

Do you like to sing? Bring a drum, and we will march in a ring, sing, and have a fling.

I like to sing and swing. What are some things that you like to do in the spring?

STORY #52

Ing   REVIEW and NEW WORDS

Sting	King	once	drum
Bing	Ping	there	what
Bring	Sing	would	said
Wing	Thing	could	bell
Ring	Wring	morning	goes
Ding	Swing	night	pretty
Jingle	bird	song	

THE KING

Once there was a king who loved to sing. He would sing in the morning, and he would sing in the night.

On day a little blue bird with two little blue wings came by. The little blue bird could sing too. The king and the bird loved to sing. They would sing all day and all night.

"What things can I bring you?" said the blue bird. "A ring, a swing, a toy drum, and a little bell that goes ping, bing, ding, jingle, jingle," said the king.

Oh, what a pretty song they would sing. They would sing, swing, play the toy drum, and ring the little jingle bell.

STORY #53

Ing   REVIEW and NEW WORDS

Bing	Sing	pong	or
Bring	Thing	party	dress
Ding	Wring	high	our
Jing	Swing	low	please
King	Spring	Queen	wear
Ping	Wing	nice	something
Ring	Fling	bee	tea
Zing	cookies	size	

A PARTY

Ping, pong went the ball. Zing, bing, ring-a-ding-a-ding went the bell. It is time to play on the swing. I can swing high. I can swing low. Here I go! Come swing and sing with me on a spring day in May.

We can play King and Queen. The Queen can bring things to the King.

He can fling a party and get a ring and a swing. What a nice thing to do. Can you dress up and come to our party? Please wear a ring and bring a hat or something, but do not bring a bee that can sting! We will have tea by the sea. I like king sized cookies too. What fun this will be for you and me.

STORY #54

Ock   REVIEW and NEW WORDS

Dock	way	fishing
Flock	large	pole
Block	want	stand
Shock	know	wait
Lock	door	their
Rock	boat	unlock

FISH BY THE DOCK

I was on my way to the dock when a large flock of birds blocked me. I was in shock. What do they want? Now, I know. They want fish. I will unlock the door to the boat dock and find my fishing pole. I will fish for the birds.

The birds stand on the rocks and wait for their fish. They like fish. The birds will stand on the rocks, by the dock and wait for their fish all day long.

STORY #55

Ock   REVIEW and NEW WORDS

Smock	tick	whopper
Block	old	surprise
Clock	head	around
Dock	chug	
Knock	road	
Rock	fish	
Lock	stand	
Unlock	over	
Shock	fishing	
Sock	pole	
Tock	catch	

A FISH STORY

Tick-tock-tick-tock goes the old clock. It is time for us to get up and rock. We put on our socks and smocks and head for the dock. Ben unlocks the door so we can go to the dock.

Knock, knock, knock goes the old truck as we chug around the block and down the road to the dock. On the dock, we fish. I love to fish. I have to stand on a block and look over a rock to see my fishing pole.

LOOK! I caught a whooper of a fish. That is a big shock! That is a big surprise! I am HAPPY!

STORY #56

Ock   REVIEW and NEW WORDS

Block	someone
Clock	water
Dock	who
Knock	there
Lock	pretty
Rock	basket
Shock	throw
Smock	how
Sock	far
Tock	very
	win

KNOCK, KNOCK

Knock, knock, knock! Someone is at the door. Unlock the door and see who is there. It is a little girl. She has a basket. In her basket, she has a block, a rock, and a clock that goes tick-tock, tick-tock.

She wants to play down by the dock. We will stand on blocks and throw rocks in the water. How far will my rock go? It will go very, very far. I will win with my rock. Lucky me!

STORY #57

Ake   REVIEW and NEW WORDS

Take	walk	playing	great
Flake	fly	scared	leap
Drake	into	three	headed
Make	bark	steps	home
Rake	snow	back	
Snake	leaves	turns	

BIG BOY

My dog, Big Boy, likes to take a walk by the lake. He can see a drake. A drake is a male duck. Big Boy can make a big bark. He likes to make the drakes fly into the sky.

He likes to play in the snow flakes and in the raked leaves. One day, as he was playing in the raked leaves, he sees a snake! He is scared. He takes three steps back, turns, and makes a great leap.

He is now headed for home. Run, Big Boy. Do not take time to play by the lake. Run from the snake as fast as you can.

STORY #58

Ake   REVIEW and NEW WORDS

Wake	Snowflake	goes
Snake	sound	Shaky
Jake	leaves	Flaky
Cake	everywhere	slice
Flake	sale	
Rake	chocolate	
Bake	milk	
Shake	home	
Take	don't	

JAKE'S SNAKE

Jake has a snake. He likes to play with his pet snake. Jake named the snake Snowflake. The snake is white with black spots. Snowflake can shake and make a funny sound. Make Snowflake, the white and black snake, shake and make a funny sound, Jake.

Jake takes Snowflake, the snake, with him to rake leaves. Jake takes Snowflake with him everywhere he goes. One day, Jake had to wake Snowflake, the snake, to take him to a cake and bake sale.

Snowflake, the snake, wanted a chocolate milk shake and a big slice of cake to take home. Jake will take the shake and the cake for him. I don't have a snake for a pet. I have a dog and a cat named Shaky and Flaky.

STORY #59

Ake REVIEW and NEW WORDS

Wake	Take	sunshine	morning	early
Snake	Shake	going	surprise	coconut
Jake	Bake	mom	making	hugs
Make		baking	dad	
Cake		some	that	
Flake		grandmother	them	
Rake		grandfather	very	
		kisses	icing	

SUNSHINE CAKE

I am going to bake a Sunshine Cake for Mom and Dad. The cake will make them very happy. The cake I bake will be a yellow cake with white icing. I will shake coconut flakes on top of the cake that I bake. I will bake the cake early in the morning. I will wake Mom and Dad with a shake, shake, shake. The Sunshine Cake will be a surprise. They will thank me for making and baking the cake.

I will take some of the Sunshine Cake to my grandmother and grandfather. They like big slices of cake. They will be happy too. They will give me kisses and hugs for my cake and call me, "Little Bake Queen."

STORY #60

Unk   REVIEW and NEW WORDS

Bunk	Rosy	animals
Drunk	pet	people
Hunk	out	tame
Junk	treats	once
Punk	sleep	
Trunk	cute	
Skunk	bed	
Chunk	own	
Sunk	Yardly	
Dunk	filled	
Stunk	perfume	
Clunk	wild	

ROSY

Little Rosy is a pet skunk. She can take a hunk out of a chunk of pet treats. She likes treats.

She sleeps in a cute little bunk bed. She has her own toy trunk. The trunk is filled with junk. Would you bunk with a skunk in a clunk of junk that stunk? Oh, no, not I.

Skunks are wild animals. Sometimes, people tame them for pets. I once had a friend who had a pet skunk named "Yardly." Yardly is the name of a perfume. That is a cute name for a skunk. She will need some perfume so she will smell good, ha, ha, ha.

STORY #61

Unk   REVIEW and NEW WORDS

Trunk	furry	head
Skunk	animal	under
Junk	bushy	sleep
Dunk	tail	water
Hunk	really	iguana
sunk	stinks	bath
Chunk	spray	soap
Drunk	phew….eeeeee	much
Stunk	home	rather

THE LITTLE SKUNK

The skunk is a cute little black and white furry animal with a big bushy tail. He looks cute, but he really stinks. He can put his tail up and spray.

Phew….eeeeee, that skunk stunk!

I had to dunk all my junk in the trunk of my truck and go home. I had to take a bath with a big chunk of soap. I had to dunk my head under the water. Then I sank down in my bunk bed and went to sleep..

I love my bunk. I love my junk. I love my truck, but I do not want a stinky, cute little skunk for a pet. I would much rather have a green iguana.

STORY #62

Unk   REVIEW and NEW WORDS

Bunk	elephant	really
Chunk	long	jump
Dunk	spray	watch
Drunk	animal	smells
Hunk	would	bet
Junk	could	everywhere
Skunk	even	
Stunk	help	
Sunk	stood	
Trunk	I'll	

THE ELEPHANT

The elephant has a very long trunk. He can dunk his trunk in the water and spray water everywhere.

He is a big hunk of an animal. I would hate to see him get stuck in some junk. I could not help him out, even if I stood on my bunk bed and gave him a chunk of chocolate candy.

I'll bet a skunk that has drunk some pop and really stunk could make him jump out of the junk. Yes, watch the elephant with the long trunk go! He is big, but he can go fast when he smells the skunk that stunk up the junk. Let's all go fast!

STORY #63

Ide   REVIEW and NEW WORDS

Bride	high	place
Glide	hand	things
Hide	far	sit
Ride	above	
Slide	earth	
Tide	ocean	
Wide	below	
Side	watch	
Pride	there	

A FUN RIDE

I like to glide high in the sky on my hang glider. I can see far and wide as I ride high above the wide earth.

I can see the ocean below. I can watch the ocean's tide come in and go out.

There is no place to hide. I can see all things far and wide. Come slide on my hang glider. Sit by my side, and I will give you a fun ride.

STORY #64

Ide   REVIEW and NEW WORDS

Bride	under
Glide	find
Hide	house
Pride	horse
Ride	hide-n-seek
Side	until
Slide	shore
Stride	anymore
Tide	
Wide	

THE BRIDE

I will hide under the wide slide. The bride will try to find me. When she finds me, we will glide as we ride down the wide slide. The bride will be by my side as we ride down the slide.

Can you slide? I like to slide. Come to my house. We will ride my horse, glide on my slide, and play hide-n-seek.

The bride can come too. She can stay until the tide comes in and the shore is not wide anymore. We will have fun.

STORY #65

Ide   REVIEW and NEW WORDS

Bride	ocean	beautiful
Glide	watch	gulls
Hide	us	lucky
Pride	joy	
Ride	early	
Side	morning	
Slide	sight	
Stride	sky	
Tide	waves	
Wide	food	

THE OCEAN

Come sit by my side on the wide slide. We can watch the ocean. The tide will come in and go out. It cannot hide from us. I like the tide. It is my pride and joy to watch the tide early in the morning and late at night.

What a beautiful sight!

The sea gulls glide high in the sky. They try to hide from us. Sometimes we watch them ride the wide waves in the ocean. The sea gulls fish in the ocean for food. The fish try to hide from the sea gulls. The sea gulls ride the wide waves and fish. Look, that sea gull got a big fat wide fish. The sea gull is lucky.

STORY #66

Ack   REVIEW and NEW WORDS

Rack	train railroad
Back	down
Black	rickety
Mack	noise
Crack	vase
Tack	carrying
Track	took
Stack	knocked
Sack	rest
Slack	ouch
Smack	sound

MACK AND THE TRAIN

The train ran down the railroad track. It made a rickety rack, rickety rack sound. The train passed by Mack's house. It made a lot of noise. It shook the house. The vase fell off the table in Mack's house. It cracked as it hit the floor.

Mack came home. He was carrying a black backpack that looked like a sack. He took off the black backpack that looked like a sack. He saw the cracked vase. He picked up the cracked vase. Then he sat down to rest.

OUCH! He sat on a tack.

That was not so funny for Mack.

STORY #67

Ack   REVIEW and NEW WORDS

Back	lunch
Black	camp
Jack	ouch
Mack	grabbed
Pack	band-aid
Rack	feels
Sack	better
Snack	never
Tack	again
track	

JACK AND MACK

Jack and Mack like to run track. They are fast. They like to camp out too. Sometimes, they will backpack. They will pack a lunch with a snack and put it in a backpack.

They like to camp and run track. One black night they camped out. Jack sat on a black tack. "OUCH!" he yelled. Mack grabbed a sack on the top rack and gave Jack a band-aid. Jack feels better now. He will never sit back on a black tack again. Never, never sit on a tack.

STORY #68

Ack   REVIEW and NEW WORDS

Back   bear
Black   snow
Jack   found
Mack   full
Pack   legs
Rack   reached
Sack   next
Snack   old
Tack
Track
Shack

THE BLACK BEAR

The big black bear made tracks in the snow. He was looking for a sack in the old shack. He found a backpack full of snacks. The backpack was high on a rack in the old shack. The big black bear stood on two legs and reached for the backpack. He grabbed a black sack full of tacks. He did not want the tacks. He wanted the snacks.

Next time, when the bear comes back to the old shack, he will get the backpack full of snacks and not the tacks. The silly, silly, big old black bear.

STORY #69

Ail   REVIEW and NEW WORDS

Bail	carry	donkey
Fail	heavy	
Frail	help	
Hail	afraid	
Jail	many	
Mail	things	
Nail	letter	
Snail	fix	
Tail	broken	
Trail	finger	
Vail	pin	

THE SNAIL

The snail could not carry the pail up the trail. It was too heavy. The snail is small and frail. He cannot carry the heavy pail up the trail. He wants to help, but he is afraid he will fail.

We can help him. We can do many things. We can mail a letter, fix a broken finger nail, play "Pin the Tail on the Donkey," and carry the pail up the trail for the frail snail.

STORY #70

Ail   REVIEW and NEW WORDS

Fail	build
Gail	boats
Mail	strong
Nail	slow
Pail	delivering
Sail	walks
Snail	long
Tail	wiggly
Wail	left
Frail	flew
Quail	away

GAIL'S DAD

Gail's dad has a pail full of nails. He likes to build boats and sails. He is strong. He is not frail. He is fast and not slow as a snail.

When Gail's dad is not nailing nails in boats, he is delivering the mail. Do you like to get mail? I like to get mail.

Gail's dad walks from house to house delivering mail. He walks down long trails. One day, he saw a snail, a quail, and a little dog with a wiggly tail. The dog ran down the trail after the snail, and the quail flew away.

STORY #71

Ail   REVIEW and NEW WORDS

Fail	Gail	Sally Nell	neighbors	painted
Mail	Nail	went	Betty Gail	each
Pail	Sail	picked	screamed	others
Snail	Trail	home	just	finger
Tail	wail	laughed	scared	friends
Frail	Quail	wrote	note	toe

SALLY NELL and BETTY GAIL

Sally Nell and Betty Gail were neighbors. Sally Nell and Betty Gail were friends. They like each other. They went down the trail with a pail. They wanted to get water in their pail.

Betty Gail saw a snail on the trail. She picked it up with a nail. Sally Nell screamed and let out a wail. She ran down the trail all the way home. Betty Gail just laughed to see Sally Nell so frail and scared of a snail on a nail.

Betty Gail wrote Sally Nell a note and put it in the mail. Now they are still friends. They play games and paint each other's finger nails and toe nails. They never did get a pail of water, and Betty Gail never again scared Sally Nell with a snail on a nail.

STORY #72

Ark   REVIEW and NEW WORDS

Bark	getting	fight
Clark	return	claws
Dark	home	
Park	path	
Parker	eyes	
Spark	arches	
Sparkle	moonlight	

PARKER IN THE PARK

It is getting very dark in the park. It is time for Clark and his dog, Parker, to return home.

On the path in the park, Parker sees a black cat with dark green eyes. Parker barks at the cat. The cat arches his back. The cat's claws sparkle in the moonlight.

Will there be a fight? Parker barks at the cat. The cat runs away. Parker runs back to Clark. "Good boy," said Clark. "It is dark. Let's go home."

STORY #73

Ark   REVIEW and NEW WORDS

Mark	bird	really
Bark	hunt	loudly
Clark	after	swim
Shark	night	
Dark	find	
Park	old	
Lark	edge	
Hark	near	

MARK and CLARK

Mark and Clark are bird dogs. They like to run and hunt. They hunt for birds. They like to hunt for larks. A lark is a bird.

Mark and Clark run in the park after dark. They bark and bark. One dark night they find an old ark on the edge of the sea. They see a shark and a lark near the ark. Mark and Clark really do bark very loudly at the shark and the lark.

Swim away, shark, swim away fast, shark. Fly away, lark, fly away fast, lark. Mark and Clark will get you!

STORY #74

Ark   REVIEW and NEW WORDS

Mark	old	coo	sounds
Clark	owl	soon	arc
Bark	oak	sun	skunks
Shark	cold	longer	bears
Dark	nap	rainbow	quails
Park	many	sky	frogs
Lark	animals	sleepy	monkeys
Hark	heard	time	rabbits
	elephants	mice	

THE OLD OWL

The old owl sat in the old oak tree in the park. It was a cold, dark night. He saw many animals and heard many sounds. He heard the bark of a dog and the coo of the lark. He saw skunks, bears, quails, frogs, monkeys, rabbits, mice, and a big fat elephant.

Soon the sun came up. It was no longer dark in the park. He saw a rainbow arc in the sky. He was sleepy. It was time for a nap in the old oak tree in the park.

Good-night, old owl.

STORY #75

Ark   REVIEW and NEW WORDS

Hark	Shark	rain	usually	indigo	only
Mark	Dark	violet	beautiful	short	after
Lark	Clark	rainbow	stand	seven	order
Bark	Park	which	know	Roy G Biv	
		neat	huh		

THE RAINBOW

Usually, after a rain, a beautiful arc will appear in the sky. It is a rainbow! It has seven beautiful colors.

The seven colors stand for ROY G BIV. This name is just made-up to help you remember the colors and the order in which the colors appear in the rainbow. Neat, huh?

Here are the colors and the order in which they appear in the sky:

R= red
O= Orange
Y= yellow
G= green
B= blue
I= indigo
V- violet

Rainbow arcs appear only for a short time. They do not appear in the dark.
Mark some marks and draw a beautiful rainbow arc. Mark the colors in the correct order.

STORY #76

Eep   REVIEW and NEW WORDS

Beep	Creep	drives	horn	owns
Deep	Jeep	farm	across	creek
Keep	Peep	when	hear	sound
Sheep	Sleep	ready	sweet	oats
Steep	Sweep	brings	Joe	

JOE'S SHEEP

Joe drives a blue jeep. The jeep's horn goes beep, beep, beep. He drives his jeep up a steep hill and across a deep creek to find his sheep. The sheep do not sleep when they hear the jeep's horn make a beep, beep, beep sound. They run to Joe's jeep. The sheep are ready to eat sweet oats. Joe brings them sweet oats in his blue jeep.

The sheep come to Joe in the jeep when they hear the horn's beep, beep, beep sound.

They are sweet little sheep.

STORY #77

Eep   REVIEW and NEW WORDS

Beep	Creep	both	from	cluck	duck
Deep	Jeep	bird	tweet	babies	quack
Peep	Weep	down	their	nest	hatch
Seep	Sheep	wait	return	bring	
Sleep	Steep	chirp	joy	joyful	

A CHICK, A BIRD AND A DUCK

A chicken, a bird, and a duck all hatch from eggs. A chicken goes cluck, cluck, cluck. A bird goes tweet, tweet, tweet. A duck goes quack, quack, quack. When they are babies, they all go peep, peep, peep.

The chick, the bird, and the duck creep down deep into their nest and sleep. They wait for their mothers to return to their nest and bring them food. When their mothers return with food, they peep, chirp, and quack for joy.

I like to hear the chickens cluck, cluck, cluck, the birds tweet, tweet, tweet and the ducks quack, quack, quack.

What a joyful day!

STORY #78

Eep   REVIEW and NEW WORDS

Beep	Steep	never	mountains	mother
Creep	Sleep	blow	over	
Deep	Sheep	horn	loud	
Jeep	Seep	along	mud	
Peep		through	forest	
Weep		drive	heard	
		Grow	it's	

MY DAD'S JEEP

My dad has a blue jeep. It is fun to ride in the jeep. We go down deep into the mud. We never get stuck. My dad lets me blow the jeep's horn.

It goes BEEP-BEEP-BEEP.

Sometimes we creep along deep into the forest. We see many animals. I heard a little baby bird go PEEP-PEEP-PEEP. It can weep for its mother. When I grow up, I am going to have a blue jeep, too. I will drive it up steep mountains and creep down on the other side of the mountain. I might see some sleepy sheep as I go down the mountain and through the deep forest.

I will have fun blowing the horn with a loud BEEP-BEEP-BEEP as I creep along in my little blue jeep.

STORY #79

Eep REVIEW and NEW WORDS

Beep	Peep	night	horn	supper
Creep	Weep	baa-baa	forest	tight
Deep	Seep	drive	find	very
Jeep	Sheep	our	them	hear
Sleep	Steep	blow	before	

MY LITTLE SHEEP

At night, my little sheep sleep. They do not weep, and they do not peep.

They go BAA- BAA-BAA.

When we drive our jeep and blow the horn with a loud BEEP-BEEP-BEEP, the sheep do not sleep. They run very fast down the steep hill. They go deep into the forest. They do not want to hear the jeep's horn with the loud BEEP-BEEP-BEEP.

We will find them before they weep. They will creep back home, have a big supper, and go to sleep.

Good-night, little sheep. Sleep tight.

STORY #80

ight   REVIEW and NEW WORDS

Bright	Right	starry	horse
Fight	Sight	moon	lit
Fright	Tight	hoot	earth
Knight	Might	branch	full
Light		whoooo	

A BRIGHT NIGHT

On a starry, starry night, when the moon is full and bright, you can see many sights. The animals like to run and play. They do not fight in the night light when the moon is full and bright.

The old hoot owl sits tight on a branch, high in a tree. He might say "Whoooo" and give the knight on a horse a fright as he rides by in the bright moon light. What a sight to see on a bright moonlit night! The animals have fun all night long. It is the right thing to do on a starry, starry night, when the moon is full, and bright, and the earth is so light.

STORY #81

Ight REVIEW and NEW WORDS

Bright	Might	last	daddy	arrived
Fight	Fright	drove	street	store
Knight	Night	asked	cone	
Light	Sight	hold	turn	
Tight	Right	next	held	

THE ICE CREAM CONE

Last night my daddy drove the car down a bright street. The street had ten bright lights.

I asked my dad for an ice cream cone. He said, "Hold on tightly, we need to take a right turn at the next bright green light." I held on tightly. I might have been frightened, but I held on tightly with all my might. When we arrived at the ice cream store on the right, I got a big chocolate nut ice cream cone. What a sight it was to see me eat that big ice cream cone on a bright light night!

STORY #82

Ump   REVIEW and NEW WORDS

Bump	Lump	about	waiting	laughed
Clump	Mump	grass	large	cold
Dump	Pump	near	piece	few
Grump	Stump	notice	cherry	pedals
Jump	Thump	bicycle	heart	

THE MUMPS

One day, when I was about five years old, I was down in the dumps, sitting on a clump of grass near a stump of a tree. I noticed a bump with a large lump on my face. I jumped up, got on my bicycle, and pumped the pedals on my bicycle as fast as I could to get home.

My mom was waiting for me with a large piece of cherry pie. I was too grumpy to eat it because I had a large lump on my face. I was frightened, and my heart was thumping. My mom just laughed and said, "You have the mumps. I will get you some cold ice cream and in a few days you will be well and not look funny with the mumps." I love my mom.

STORY #83

Ump   REVIEW and NEW WORDS

Bump	Lump	foot	bad	sheet
Clump	Mump	landed	need	dozen
Dump	Pump	head	deed	shapes
Grump	Stump	kicked	hard	batch
Jump	Hump	threw	batch	chip
Thump	dirt	dough		

MY LITTLE RABBIT

I have a little rabbit. He can jump, jump, jump. He can take his little foot and thump, thump, thump.

One day, my little rabbit jumped over a stump and landed with a bump, bump, bump. Oh, what a grumpy little rabbit was he, with a lump and a bump on his head. He kicked at a stump; he threw a clump of dirt and said, "What a bad little rabbit am I. I need to do a good deed."

So, he jumped up and ran home. He worked very hard to make a batch of chocolate chip cookies. He dumped a clump of dough on the cookie sheet. He made cookie shapes and put the cookies in the oven to bake. He made two dozen chocolate chip cookies for his mother. What a sweet little rabbit that can jump, thump and cook!

STORY #84

	REVIEW and NEW WORDS
Ab	
Cab	together
Crab	everywhere
Dab	lunch
Grab	everyday
Jab	work
Lab	job
Nab	
Scab	
Tab	

THE CRABBY CRAB

I had to grab a cab on my way to the lab. I work at the lab. I jab and dab in this and that at my job. Once I colored a crab purple. He was very crabby about that.

I put a tab on him in the lab. He did not even like that. I had to give him candy and a nab. He grabbed me and made a scab. He is a very crabby crab, but I still like him.

I will never color him purple, and he will never grab me. We now ride together everywhere we go in the big yellow cab. We grab a dab of lunch every day on the way to the lab. The crab and I are friends.

STORY #85

Ab   REVIEW and NEW WORDS

Cab	Jab	named	yummy	won't
Crab	Lab	paper	teeth	vending
Dab	Nab	chase	tasty	machine
Gab	Scab	paws	treat	
Grab	Tab	creek	nose	

MY LAB

I have a big black lab named Tab. He can grab the morning paper and chase the yellow cab. He likes to dab to cab. He likes to dab his paws in the creek looking for a yummy crab to jab his teeth into for a tasty treat. Sometimes, my lab just grabs them with his teeth. One day a big crab grabbed him and made a scab on his nose. He was a funny looking lab with a scab on his nose.

Now he won't dab his paws in the creek looking for a crab. We just go down to the vending machine and hit a tab for candy and some nabs. My lab, Tab, likes nabs and candy now, not crabs.

STORY #86

Ag REVIEW and NEW WORDS

Bag	Rag	early	clean	before
Drag	Sag	large	much	finally
Flag	Snag	feed	next	decided
Gag	Tag	stall	help	really
Nag	Wag	tried	neighbor	melted

THE GOOD NAG

Early every morning, the little old man dragged a large bag of feed to the horse stall to feed his nag. A nag is a horse.

One day, his bag got snagged on a tag, and all his nag's feed fell out. He tried to clean it up with a rag, but it was just too much. He got his dog, Wag, and tried to get him to eat the nag's feed, but Wag didn't like nag's feed. He just gagged when he tried to eat the feed.

Next, he tried to flag down a neighbor for help, but his neighbor had a big bag of ice and had to get home before the ice melted.

Finally, he decided to get his nag and let him eat it up. The old nag really liked the feed and ate it all up. He is a good fat old nag now.

STORY #87

Ag REVIEW and NEW WORDS

Bag	Rag	American	neck	use
Drag	Sag	flying	collar	dirt
Flag	Snag	front	think	road
Gag	Tag	our	might	sight
Nag	Wag	games	beautiful	wait

I LIKE SCHOOL

We have an American flag flying in front of our school. I like to go to school and play games. We play tag. We drop a rag and run. It is fun to drop a rag and run.

One day, I took a beautiful rag in my bag. I wanted to use it when we played tag, but it fell out of my bag, and I dragged it down the dirt road. It was a sad sight to see. Now, what will we use for a rag to play tag? Wait, I see Wags, our pet dog, coming down the street with a rag collar on his neck. Do you think Wags will let us use his collar? I hope so. It will be fun to play tag with his rag collar. We might let Wags run around the flag pole and play tag too. That will be fun and a nice thing to do.

STORY #88

Ad   REVIEW and NEW WORDS

Bad	Lad	once	met	most
Chad	Mad	rough	mountains	great
Dad	Pad	road	would	
Glad	Sad	popcorn	air	
Had	Tad	mattress	relaxes	

TAD

Tad is a lad who was sad. Once he met my dad, Chad, Tad was very glad. They always had fun. They would ride horses over bad rough mountain roads. After that, they were glad to have a pad to sit on so they would not be sad.

The lad and my dad had many days of fun. They were always happy and never mad or sad. Tad and Chad are friends. I am glad because Tad is my friend too. We like to eat popcorn and watch TV on my glad pad. Dad likes my glad pad also. He relaxes with us and watches TV. He eats most of the popcorn, but we still think he is a great dad.

STORY #89

Ad   REVIEW and NEW WORDS

Bad	Lad	tadpole	aunt	uncle	pond
Chad	Mad	behind	house	visit	tail
Dad	Pad	older	lily	croak	hear
Glad	Sad	finally	grew	lost	Taddy
Had	Tad	disappear			

THE SAD LITTLE TADPOLE

My aunt and uncle have a big pond behind their house. When I visit them, I go down to the pond with my friend Chad. We look for tadpoles. Do you know what a tadpole is? It is a cute little baby frog with a tail.

This little tadpole was sad, bad, and mad because he wanted to be a frog. He did not want to be a tadpole. When he gets older, he will be glad because his tail will disappear and he will become a frog. He will sit on a lily pad and croak. Dad, to croak. Dad, Chad, my aunt and uncle, and I can hear the frogs croaking at night. The sound makes me glad.

Chad and I named this little tadpole Taddy. He finally grew up and lost his tail. Now he sits on the lily pads and croaks with all the big glad frogs in the pond.

STORY #90

Oke   REVIEW and NEW WORDS

Broke	Spoke	a lot	ingredients	batter
Coke	Stroke	oven	sudden	watching
Joke	Woke	ok	burning	neighbors
Poke	Yoke	truth	saved	pieces
Smoke	Choke	really	another	together

MOTHER'S CAKE

My mother likes to bake. She baked a cake using a lot of eggs, flour, and other ingredients. Eggs have whites and yolks inside the shell. The yolks are yellow. She broke the eggs and the shells into the cake batter. This is no joke. She really did! I was watching her and drinking Coke as she put the cake in the oven to bake. All of a sudden, I got choked on my Coke. Mother stroked me on my back, and I was ok.

What do I see? What do I smell? It is smoke. Oh, no, mother's cake is burning! The smoke is choking me. Let's not poke around. Let's get out of here!

Mother woke up the neighbors and together they put out the fire. We saved the house, but the cake was black and broken into pieces. We will have to bake another cake. Really, this is the truth and no joke.

STORY #91

Oke   REVIEW and NEW WORDS

Broke	Smoke	stubborn	donkey	bribe
Coke	Stroke	decided	moving	slowly
Choke	Spoke	gush	blew	reared
Joke	Woke	gear	flew	bottle
Poke	Yoke	collar	anymore	

POKEY THE DONKEY

The old donkey just poked along. I spoke to him and tried to get him to move fast. Finally, I poked him and spoke to him, but he was stubborn and would not move fast.

I put a yoke on his neck. A yoke is a collar to put around an animal's neck. I even tried to bribe him with a Coke, but still he just poked along.

To get him to go fast must just be a joke.

He would not drink the Coke, so I decided to drink it. We were moving along very slowly when a big gush of wind blew smoke into his nose. He reared up, put his body in gear, and away we flew at a fast rate. He was running so fast that I dropped my Coke and broke the Coke bottle. No joke, this little donkey can really move when he gets choked on smoke. I cannot call him "Pokey" anymore.

STORY #92

Eat   REVIEW and NEW WORDS

Beat	Meat	vacation	hamburger	Florida
Cheat	Neat	earth	real	grow
Cleat	Seat	cereal	can't	heard
Eat	Treat	lunch	ordered	cold
Heat	Wheat	thought	year	plants

A FAMILY VACATION

My family and I went on a vacation. It was fun. We went to Florida for some fun and sun. The sun gives heat to the earth. Warm sun is a real treat on a cold day. It also helps wheat and all other plants to grow. We make bread from wheat. We also make cereal from wheat. I like to eat things made from wheat. You just can't beat a good wheat treat. Our car has heat in the seats. Have you ever heard of that? Oh, yes, it is really true. Well, the seats and everything in the car were getting hot from the heat, so we stopped to get cool and to get some lunch. I ordered a hamburger with meat to eat. I also ordered a cold strawberry milk shake to cool off from the heat. I thought cooling off was a neat thing to do.

Maybe next year, you can go on a vacation with us. I hope you can

STORY #93

Eat   REVIEW and NEW WORDS

Beat	Meat	brother	football	possibilities
Cheat	Neat	star	actually	Wheaties
Cleat	Seat	uniform	traction	sport
Eat	Treat	fair	season	cotton
Heat	Wheat	team	other	sweet

MY BROTHER

My brother is a big football star. He eats Wheaties. He thinks he is cool and neat. Actually, I do too. He has a uniform. He has cleats in his shoes. The cleats help him to have traction and reduce the possibilities of his sliding down.

He never cheats when he plays football. To cheat is not being a good sport. Fair play is the name of the game.

My family has season seats. We always know where we will sit. We yell for our team. We hope we beat the other team. At the games, we order hot dogs and hamburgers filled with good meat to eat. Then we get a sweet cotton candy treat.

My brother is a good player. It is neat to have a big brother so sweet.

STORY #94

Am   REVIEW and NEW WORDS

Clam	Gram	soup	decided	straighten	
Ham	Sam	invite	brought	tomorrow	
Jam	Slam	honey	except	crackers	
Pam	Swam	finger	accident	delicious	
Ram	Yam	key	better	able	which

CLAM DIGGING

Gram, Sam, and Pam like to dig for clams. Clams are good to eat. Sam's mother makes clam soup, which is really delicious! One day, they decided to have a party and invite all their friends for a clam bake. Some friends brought ham; some brought jam with yams, and some brought Honey Graham Crackers. They played games and had a lot of food to eat.

Everyone had a nice time, except Sam. He had an accident just before he left the party. Someone slammed the car door on his finger. It was jammed in the door. His father rammed the car key into the door and was able to unlock the door.

We think Sam's finger is going to be ok. It looks a little crooked, but we think it will straighten out.

Tomorrow, if Sam's finger is better, we will all go clam digging.

Pam made Sam a sandwich. She put ham, jam, clams, and yams on it -- yuck! I just like peanut butter and jam on my sandwich. Sometimes, I make a mustard and ham sandwich. It is good too.

STORY #95

Am   REVIEW and NEW WORDS

Clam	Ram	sandwich	peanut	mustard	across
Gram	Sam	picnic	swim	pool	delightful
Ham	Slam	through	house	course	shade
Jam	Swam	lazy	arrived	packed	dessert
Pam	Yam	summer	many	found	afternoon

THE PICNIC

Pam and Sam were going to the park for a picnic and an afternoon swim. They were in a hurry. They ran as fast as they could through the house, rammed into the wall, and slammed the door. Running, ramming, and slamming, of course, were not good things to do.

Finally, they arrived at the park. The park was jammed packed with many people. Pam and Sam found some friends. They swam across the swimming pool and then found a nice shade tree to sit under. They ate their sandwiches and had Graham Crackers with peanut butter for dessert. It was a good dessert.

Eating dessert was a delightful way to spend a lazy summer afternoon.

STORY #96

Ap	REVIEW and NEW WORDS				
Cap	Nap	circus	house	needed	hair
Clap	Slap	our	way	excited	nose
Flap	Snap	fingers	bought	popcorn	shoes
Lap	Tap	sodas	tried	activity	
Map	Trap	clowns	large	cherry	

THE CIRCUS

We went to the circus. It was far from our house. Mom and Dad needed a map to find our way.

I was so excited that I tapped my feet. I clapped my hands and snapped my fingers. I knew that this was going to be a fun day. There were many people at the circus. We finally found our seats. My little brother had to sit in my lap so he could see all the activity at the circus. He wanted to see the animals and the funny clowns.

Mom and Dad bought us popcorn, cotton candy, sodas and funny looking caps. We had a great day. I liked watching all the animals do funny tricks. The clowns were fun to watch also. They had very large shoes, crazy hair of all colors, and big cherry noses.

I hope we can go to the circus next year. Do you think we will need a map?

STORY #97

Ap   REVIEW and NEW WORDS

Cap	Nap	bang	enormous	though
Clap	Slap	please	save	where
Flap	Snap	crazy	quickly	open
Lap	Tap	turned	around	yeah
Map	Trap	catch	trying	

THE FUNNY CRAZY BEAR

Bang! Clap! Snap! Do you hear me tapping on the trap door? Let me in, let me in the trap door. An enormous black crazy bear with a funny cap is trying to trap me and catch me in the woods.

He does crazy things. I think he came from the circus. He can do funny tricks. I saw him clap and snap his paws. He turned around and around trying to catch his tail. Then, I saw him flap his ears and tap his head. I think he is trying to trap me. I think he wants me to sit on his lap and tap and clap, but I really don't want to sit on his lap, and clap. So, please let me in the trap door. Save me from the funny black bear. He is crazy! Here he comes with a rap, tap, tap as he claps, claps, claps. He knows where I am, and he doesn't even need a map. Open the trap door quickly! Oh, thank you for opening the trap door. Now, the bear can bang, clap, snap, slap, and try to get through the flap on the trap door. He can't get through the flap on the trap door. He can't get me now. Yeah!

STORY #98

Est   REVIEW and NEW WORDS

Best	Pest	fierce	uninvited	robin	beckon
Chest	Rest	breast	beautiful	flew	prevail
Crest	Test	edge	spread	lovely	protect
Guest	Vest	puffed	rising	course	brave
Nest	West	mean	arrived	chirp	brave

LITTLE ROB

Little Robin Red Breast flew to a tree on the edge of the crest. She spread out her lovely wings and puffed out her chest. She had just had a good night's rest and was ready for a beautiful day. Her three little babies were resting in the nest. The morning sun was rising in the East. Of course, you know that the sun rises in the East and sets in the West.

In the meantime, a fierce pest arrived at the nest. He was an uninvited guest. The babies did their best to chirp loudly. They needed to beckon their mother for help. Mother Robin Red Breast heard their cry for help. She flew very fast to the nest to protect her babies. They were being brave waiting for her to get to the nest. She was able to fight off the big fierce uninvited pest from the West. It was a test of bravery. She saved her babies in the nest.

Now, the sun was setting in the West. It was time to rest. Mother Robin Red Breast fluffed her feathers and gathered her little babies under her wings as the sun disappeared over the crest. It had been an exciting day! Not always do the big and fierce win, but often the little and brave prevail. Always do your best.

STORY #99

Est   REVIEW and NEW WORDS

Best	Pest	gorilla`	rain	forest	smart
Chest	Rest	expression	tools	blooded	build
Crest	Test	connect	blade	mammals	pizza
Guest	Vest	rods	grass	whole	facial
Nest	West	intelligent	quotient		reaching

GORILLAS

The gorillas of the rain forest are large brave animals. They are mammals just like you and me. They have hair. They are born alive. They are warm-blooded, and their babies drink milk. They have cute little facial expressions. They take care of each other. The big ones, and even some of the little ones, stand up and beat on their chest. I think they want the whole forest, from north, south, east and west to know that they are the best.

Gorillas have a rather high intelligent quotient (IQ). They know how to use tools. They can connect two rods together and make a long reaching tool to get something that is out of their reach. They love termites. They get a long blade of grass and poke it down into a termite hill. They slowly bring it out of the termite hill and eat all the termites that are stuck to the blade of grass. Pretty smart, huh! Would you like to have lunch with a gorilla? Yuck! No, thanks, I would rather have a pizza. Pizzas are the best from the North, South, East or West.

Gorillas like to rest in nests that they build in trees. They play and look for food all day. Late in the evening, as the sun sets over the crest in the West, they know it is time to rest. Good night, gorillas. Sleep tight in your tree nest.

STORY #100

Ore   REVIEW and NEW WORDS

Wore	Shore	straw	shoes	hole
Chore	Snore	imagine	attire	local
More	Sore	general	desire	found
Pore	Tore	piece	found	afternoon
Score	Bore	secret	grown	especially
		promise	finish	

PAW PAW

There was an old man who lived down by the shore. He was a rather funny looking old man in his floppy straw hat, short pants, and old worn shoes. He tore holes in his shoes because the shoes made his toes sore. He had more holes in his shirt than you can imagine. Even with his funny attire, everyone loved him and called him "Paw Paw."

One warm lazy afternoon, the children went to Paw Paw's store and found him sound asleep. He was snoring! He did not know he was snoring because he was asleep. Do you snore?

The children decided not to wake him. They would let him snore away the afternoon. They never, never told anyone that Paw Paw snores. Will you promise to keep it a secret too?

All the children, who lived down by the shore with Paw Paw, are grown now, but they still go to visit the old man by the shore who wears a floppy straw hat, short pants, and old worn shoes...

Story 100 is dedicated to my husband, Charles C. Lavender.